Gratitude

Gratitude

Inspirations by Melody Beattie
Author of *The Language of Letting Go*

Art by Jane Mjolsness

HAZELDEN

Hazelden
Center City, Minnesota 55012-0176

1-800-328-0094
1-651-213-4590 (Fax)
www.hazelden.org

Library of Congress Cataloging-in-Publication Data

Beattie, Melody.
    Gratitude : inspirations / by Melody Beattie.
       p. cm.
    ISBN-13: 978-1-59285-408-0 (softcover)
1.   Gratitude—Religious aspects—Meditations. I. Title.
    BL65.G73.B43 2007
    158.1 8—dc22   2006049737
       '2

Editor's note
The text in this book has been adapted from *More Language of Letting Go*
by Melody Beattie.

11   10   09   6 5 4 3 2

Cover and interior design by David Spohn
Cover illustration by Jane Mjolsness
Typesetting by Prism Publishing Center

Introduction

In our busy, harried lives, it's tempting to focus on what we haven't accomplished and what we don't yet possess. That trap of *more, more, more* only alienates us from our loved ones and our connectedness with a Higher Power. The solution to reconnecting to what's important in life can be as simple as getting in touch with the power of gratitude.

With practice, it is possible to redirect our focus from large, daunting problems to life's small, beautiful blessings that are ever present and ever sustaining.

Cultivating a true sense of gratitude is more than counting our blessings and saying thank you for what's good. When we're learning to speak the language of gratitude, we learn to say thank you for everything in our lives, whether we feel grateful or not. That's how we turn around circumstances that frustrate or disappoint us.

The benefits of nurturing an attitude of gratitude are numerous. A sense of gratitude immediately gives us a sense of perspective when facing problems. Gratitude helps us make the most of resources at hand. And above all else, a sense of gratitude helps us truly recognize the presence of a Higher Power in our lives.

When we hoard what we have been given, we block the door to receiving more. If you are feeling stagnant in your life, share some of what has been given to you. Let go of some of the sorrow that you have experienced by sharing your experience—and the compassion that you have learned from it—with another. Share your success by teaching someone else your methods. Share in the abundance given to you; donate to a favorite charity or church. Give of your time, your money, your abilities. When you give, you open the door to receive more.

Someone once asked the artist Georgia O'Keeffe why her paintings magnified the size of small objects—like the petals on a flower—making them appear larger than life, and reduced the size of large objects—like mountains—making them smaller than life.

"Everyone sees the big things," she said. "But these smaller things are so beautiful and people might not notice them if I didn't emphasize them." That's the way it is with gratitude and letting go. It's easy to see the problems in our lives. They're like mountains. But sometimes we overlook the smaller things; we don't notice how truly beautiful they are.

God, teach me how to enjoy and savor the pleasures, gifts, and talents that are spread out before me.

Be grateful you're where you are at this moment.

Don't worry about trying to hurry the future along.

Look for the joy in life now.

Let yourself have all your emotions and feelings about losing people and moments you loved and cherished. Feel as sad as you need to. Grieve. Then let the feelings and the past go. Don't let your memories stop you from seeing how beautiful and precious each moment in your life is now.

God, thank you
for what I've been given.

God, help me give abundantly of what's been given to me. Teach me how to give, so that both my giving and my receiving are healthy and free from attachments.

God, please help me let go of my expectations and accept the gifts that you give me each day, knowing that there is beauty and wonder in each act of life.

It's so easy to see and notice what we like in other people. Sometimes, it's not as easy to see the attributes and beauty in ourselves. It's good to see the beauty in others. But sometimes, take a moment and get excited when you notice what's beautiful in yourself, too.

Take another look at that moment when one door has closed behind you and you're standing in that dark hallway, but no door opens up. Perhaps you have let go of whatever you've been grasping so tightly and you're left standing with an empty hand. If you're at an in-between place, don't just accept it. Revel in it, embrace it, rejoice at your opportunity to sit in the birthplace of all that will come along your path. Relax into the void and allow creation to flow.

God, help me see the beauty and the good in life. Help me be aware of what I like in others, so that I can better define what I aspire to become.

God, help me welcome all the new experiences in my life. Give me the courage to calmly walk my path today, knowing I'm right where I need to be.

In our everyday lives, there are times when we are frightened, times when we need a friend to give us courage, and times when we can be a friend giving courage to someone else. Be grateful for those who have helped you find strength. Be grateful for the times when you have helped your friends find courage of their own.

Sometimes, we can sit down and anticipate the times to come. We can look at our money, our strength, our abilities, our stamina, and say wearily, "There just won't be enough." That's because we're looking too far ahead. Look around at what you have available, this moment or this hour. Use the resources and gifts you've been given. Tomorrow's manna will come at its appointed hour.

God, grant me the
serenity that acceptance brings.

God, help me accept all the twists
and turns along my path.
Help me learn to be present to the
good and the unfortunate incidents
that come my way.

When we want something so badly—for instance our spouse to change, or that job, or that woman or that man—we begin to obsess and dwell. We take ourselves out of that place of balance and end up in a no-win tailspin. Don't let your needs and desires run away with you. Yes, passion is great stuff. Identify what you want. Then let it go. And ask God what your lesson is.

We can want things, pray for things, and hope that things will come to pass. But ultimately, we're not in control. Instead of spending our time and energy trying to get someplace else, we can learn the lesson and enjoy the beauty of the life we've been given.

Are you focusing on the circumstances of your life instead of the lessons? Instead of asking why, learn to ask what the lesson is. The moment you become ready to accept it, the lesson will become clear.

God, help me be clear with you and myself about what I really want. Then, help me let go of my intentions and surrender to your plan.

Today, I will come back to balance with any need or want that seems to be controlling my life. Instead of dwelling on it, I'll give it to God and focus on taking care of myself.

We call it keeping up with the Joneses. They buy a boat and we buy a bigger one. They get a new TV and we get a big screen. While it helps to identify with each other, we're not all the same. So why compare ourselves on the basis of material things?

God, help me learn to enjoy the people and experiences in my life.

God, help me to quiet my noisy,
worrisome mind in my ordinary world.
Help me to relax in the familiar and
to be aware of and appreciate it.

Wanting what we can't have is a universal dilemma. It's so easy to conjure up fantasies about how delicious it would be if we could only have *that*, even though we know we never could. Then we don't have to deal with what we have. Learn to recognize longing and yearning for what we can't have.

Make a list of everything in your life that you're *not* grateful for. You may not have to make a list; you probably have the things that bother you memorized. Then deliberately practice gratitude for everything on the list. The power of gratitude won't let you down. Being grateful for whatever we have always turns what we have into more.

God, show me the power of gratitude.
Help me make it a regular, working
tool in my life.

Sometimes in life we can't get what we want. Other times, we can. And sometimes the journey to getting there is full of twists and turns, much more of an adventure than anything we could have planned.

It's important to be grateful. But sometimes, repressing our emotions and not saying how we feel about a situation is a form of trying to control the situation, too. We think if we hold our breath, don't complain, and do everything right, the universe will just benevolently give us what we want. Is there a situation in your life that you've been hoping would magically get better if you bit your lip and wished long enough? If you've started playing the waiting game in a particular situation, tell yourself how you really feel.

We can't relax when we're being judgmental. As soon as we decide that a thing or situation is either good or bad, we place ourselves in the situation of having to do something about it. For example, if someone is good, we begin to compare ourselves to that person: *Am I better or worse? What can I do to improve?* If we decide that a thing is bad, then our conscience tells us that we must try to get rid of it. Either way, we get so busy thinking about our judgments and allowing our minds to create scenarios that we cannot relax and enjoy things the way they are.

Become conscious as you go through your daily life. Go on a treasure hunt. Find out what feels good to you. You just might discover that there are more treasures and pleasures in this world than you thought.

God, teach me to use gratitude and letting go to reduce the size of my problems.

When people suggest being grateful, it's easy to think that means counting our blessings and just saying thank you for what's good. When we're learning to speak the language of letting go, however, we learn to say thanks for everything in our lives, whether we feel grateful or not. That's how we turn things around.

*God, help me be
grateful for all the problems and
circumstances in my life.*

It's easy to be thankful for answered prayers, easy to be joyfully grateful when the universe gives us exactly what we want. What's not so easy is to remember to be grateful when we don't get what we want.

God, thank you for the resistance in my life. Help me to stop fighting with it and to use that energy to truly solve the problem.

Sometimes when we pray, we get what we want. Sometimes we get what we need. Accept both answers—the yes's and the something else's—with heartfelt gratitude. Then look around and see what your lesson and gift are.

When problems and challenges arise, they force us to examine our ideals, become alert, and often learn something new about others and ourselves. Even our enemies, rivals, and competitors give us something to push against. They help us define who we are and challenge us to become our best. Instead of complaining and grumbling about a problem or circumstance, thank it for being there.

*God, thank you for not always giving
me what I think is best.*

Remember to be grateful.
God doesn't owe us anything.
All of it is a gift.

Sometimes we get what we pray for. Sometimes we don't. Be grateful—force gratitude; fake it if you must—when God answers your furtive prayers by saying no. Take the rejections with a smile. Let God's "no's" move you happily down the road. Maybe you're not being punished, after all. Maybe God is protecting you from yourself.

Don't get bitter or so involved with feeling blue about not getting what you requested that you miss out on what you did receive. Wants and needs are closely connected. And all our needs, even the ones we're not completely aware of yet, will be met. Be grateful that God knows more about what we need than we do.

God, help me remember to be thankful even when the gift is not quite what I expected.

God, help me to laugh, cry, love, be aware, and be thankful with all my heart for every moment and each experience that I've been given. Thank you for my life.

Practice an act of gratitude. Find one of your guiding lights or guardian angels and tell that person what he or she means to you in your life. Your guides may not even be aware of the impact that they have had on you. And who knows whether your kind words may be just the light that they need today to push them gently down their path with heart.

Then, take it one step further. Take the kind, loving thing they did to or for you and pass it along to someone else.

God, thank you for the people I resent and envy. Bless them richly. Open doors for them, shower them with abundance. Help me know that my success doesn't depend on their failure; it's equivalent to how much I ask you to bless them.

God, thank you for the past.
Help me let go with gratitude,
so that I can live more fully
and joyfully now.

Could it be that you're who you are and where you are now for a reason? Thank God for your life, exactly as it is, right now.

God, thanks for everything,

just as it is.

Are you grateful for each experience you've had? Are you grateful for the story you're living now? The good news is, the story of your life hasn't ended yet. There's still more to come. Touch the experience of being human in all of its sorrow and joy.

Be grateful for the story you're living now.

Remember, there's a difference between knowing about the power of gratitude and actually applying gratitude in your life.

God, thank you for the ability and desire to love. Love is a cherished gift from you.

We can feel good about the things we've done, the part we've played in taking care of our lives. But remember, healing is a gift. So is love. So is success. Feel good about doing your part in helping yourself. But a gentle thank you to God may be in order, too.

Are you grateful for the people you live with? Or, if you live alone, are you grateful for your friends? The great thing about being independent is that we get to choose our families. Be thankful for your family today, whether it's the one that you were born with or the one that you've chosen. Our families are a gift.

God, thank you for my families.

God, remind me to give
thanks where thanks is due.

Sometimes, the last thin cord binding us to a person, an experience, or a part of our lives that we're trying so valiantly to be free from, can be effectively snipped with the shears of gratitude.

Part of saying *thanks* is sharing our lives with the world. The other part is learning to enjoy our lives, ourselves. Live and love and learn and see things; then pass those things on. Don't just say *thanks*. Demonstrate your gratitude for life by living as fully as you can.

If you've been given much, be thankful. Use your abundance wisely. Enjoy it. Share it with others. Be thankful for the gifts in your life.

Celebrate the abundance that comes into your life. So often we spend so long in the "do without" stage that we don't know what to do when we're given the opportunity to "do with."

Friendship is an important gift from God. Don't just tell your friends how much they mean in your life. Show your friends how much you care with an act of gratitude.

God, thank you for making each of us unique. Thank you for my friends.

*Make a commitment to
show your gratitude by sharing
it with others whenever you
have the opportunity.*

Gratitude is a form of self-expression that must be shared. We cannot have an attitude of gratitude without having an object of that gratitude.

Today, celebrate who you are. Yes, you have much in common with other people. But you're also uniquely you. Instead of fussing and worrying about how different you are, be grateful that you're unique. Celebrate being you.

We cannot show gratitude without sharing it with someone. When we show our gratitude, it's a way of sharing our joy with that person. Even when we do something as simple as burning a candle to show our gratitude to God, it shares our joy with everyone who sees the flame of the candle. It strengthens their faith and reminds them to show their gratitude, too.

Demonstrate gratitude in your actions every day. Gratitude is more than just a thought process and more than just a Sunday-morning church activity. Demonstrate your gratitude through your compassion and your tolerance.

Sometimes we get so busy
trying to get more, we forget to be
thankful for what we've got.

We can show our gratitude for life in even our smallest actions. Find a way to demonstrate your gratitude to the universe. Action gives life to ideas. When we start to look for ways to show our gratitude, we will find more and more to be grateful for.

Make showing and sharing your gratitude a part of your life. If someone does something nice for you, share your happiness with that person. Send a card or make a phone call. If you believe that a prayer has been answered by God, share your gratitude with God. Tell someone, or thank God publicly at your worship service. If you have had a victory in your life, show your gratitude by sharing it with others.

*God, today I will show you
how grateful I am.*

Here's an interesting phenomenon about gratitude: it's difficult to feel bad when we're feeling grateful. The mind has room for only one thought at a time. If we fill it with gratitude, there isn't room for negativity.

Today, be grateful for your life. Allow that gratitude to carry over into your activities and to flavor all of your interactions. Think of one thing to be grateful about in each activity you do, with each person you interact with, and in each task that you do. Find the gratitude in your life, and you'll find joy standing right next to it.

Comparison is judgmental. We judge this to be better than that, and this to be worse than the other. By comparing and judging, we deny ourselves the beauty of the moment and the wonder of the life that's in front of us now. Instead of deciding if a situation is good or bad, just be thankful for it—the way it is.

God, thank you for every detail of my ordinary, everyday world.

If comparing and judging is draining all the joy out of your life, start putting some fun back in it by applying a little gratitude instead.

God, thank you for all my victories, for all the challenges you've helped me meet. Thanks for all those times you answered my prayers and met my needs. Help me rest and celebrate the good in my life.

If instead of seeing the beautiful horizon or the clouds, all you can see is down, apply gratitude and humility to each aspect of your life.

God, help me use the powerful remedy of gratitude as a tool for daily transformation in my life.

Sometimes, the best way to say thanks is to simply enjoy with humble confidence the gifts and pleasures that are offered to us today.

Look closely at the ordinary in your life. While you're being grateful, don't forget to express pure, sheer gratitude for how beautiful the ordinary really is. We can easily overlook the ordinary and take it for granted. The sun rises and sets, the seasons come and go, and we forget how beautiful and sensational the familiar really is.

Reflect on your past successes. Forget about your failures and the things that went wrong. Think about all that you've done right in your life, the things that have worked out, the answered prayers. Don't just stare at your problems and everything that's gone wrong. Look at what's right in your life, too.

*God, please help me to accept
all the life-changing experiences
that I may have. Help me to see
the wonder in rebirth and to
learn your lessons.*

God, help me celebrate all my triumphs. Thank you for walking with me, even when I felt like I was walking alone.

There are a lot of afflicted streams out there: greed, envy, negativity, regret, revenge, resentment, arrogance, victimization, hard-heartedness, bitterness, control, hatred. An afflicted stream is more than an isolated emotion. It's a position, a posture, an attitude, a pattern that will poison us and our lives. Feeling restless, irritable, and discontented is definitely an afflicted stream. If you find yourself in that stream, step right out into gratitude.

We each have different gifts and pleasures available at any given time in our lives. Sometimes, we have to look to see what these gifts are. The pleasures may be as simple as a view of an old oak tree from our kitchen window, a big bathtub that fills up with hot water and comforts our body and soul, or a walk around the city block surrounding the apartment we rent.

Families and parents come in all different kinds.
Be grateful for the good passed on to you
from your ancestors and your heritage.

God, help me to not take anything for granted. Teach me to recognize, appreciate, and celebrate the ordinary in this world. Help me see how beautiful and meaningful the ordinary really is.

It's easy to take many things in our life for granted: health, a loved one, friends, and food. When life proceeds smoothly, it's easy to take the ordinary for granted. Look at the ordinary in your life. How would you feel if it was taken away? Don't just be grateful for successes. Be grateful and celebrate the ordinary in your world.

*God, heal my heart toward
all my family members. Help me
accept each person for who he or
she is. Then help me genuinely
accept myself, too.*

Experience is the privilege of being human. I can taste the spaghetti. I can smell the salt of the ocean. I can feel the burning cedar taking the chill out of the air. I can love. I can hurt. What a sweet experience this is. And I thank God for every moment and feeling of each experience I've been given.

Don't get angry when the time comes in your life to let someone or something go. Open your heart to that person, place, or thing, and say, "Thanks for teaching me to love and helping me to grow." Then let go, without resentment in your heart.

Take a moment. Review where you've been for the past year. Be grateful for all you've experienced and the people who have come into your life. Search your heart. Let go of any resentments. Take a moment and reflect on your successes. Be grateful for them; be grateful for all the ordinary moments, too.

"When we have a toothache, we know that not having a toothache is happiness. But later, when we don't have a toothache, we don't treasure our non-toothache," Thich Nhat Hanh gently reminds us in his book *The Heart of the Buddha's Teaching*. Take another look at your ordinary world. See how glorious it is.

God, help me find at least one thing
in my life that makes me feel good and
gives me pleasure, even if it's for only
one moment of my day.

Remember,
love is a gift from God.

It's so easy to get hooked into the busyness of life. It's easy to focus on the destination and tell ourselves we'll be happy when we get there and forget to be happy and cherish the beauty of each moment of the trip. So often, we don't even know that we're living the best, most beautiful part of our lives right now.

You might not be going through a time in your life that you relish, but try to find a few moments where you can catch your breath, look around, and say, "How sweet it is."

*God, help me let go of my
expectations and delight in what is.*

No matter what time it is,
it's never too late to say thanks
and have a good day.

Hazelden Publishing is a division of the Hazelden Foundation, a not-for-profit organization. Since 1949, Hazelden has been a leader in promoting the dignity and treatment of people afflicted with the disease of chemical dependency.

The mission of the foundation is to improve the quality of life for individuals, families, and communities by providing a national continuum of information, education, and recovery services that are widely accessible; to advance the field through research and training; and to improve our quality and effectiveness through continuous improvement and innovation.

Stemming from that, the mission of this division is to provide quality information and support to people wherever they may be in their personal journey—from education and early intervention, through treatment and recovery, to personal and spiritual growth.

Although our treatment programs do not necessarily use everything Hazelden publishes, our bibliotherapeutic materials support our mission and the Twelve Step philosophy upon which it is based. We encourage your comments and feedback.

The headquarters of the Hazelden Foundation are in Center City, Minnesota. Additional treatment facilities are located in Chicago, Illinois; Newberg, Oregon; New York, New York; Plymouth, Minnesota; and St. Paul, Minnesota. At these sites, we provide a continuum of care for men and women of all ages. Our Plymouth facility is designed specifically for youth and families.

For more information on Hazelden, please call **1-800-257-7800**. Or you may access our World Wide Web site on the Internet at **www.hazelden.org**.

OTHER TITLES THAT MAY INTEREST YOU

The Language of Letting Go
Melody Beattie
The author integrates her own life experiences and fundamental recovery reflections in this unique daily meditation book. Softcover, 408 pp.
Order No. 5076

More Language of Letting Go
366 New Daily Meditations by Melody Beattie
Melody Beattie
Melding essays and meditations, this book offers the best-selling author's reflections on the joys and challenges that relationships present every day. Softcover, 432 pp.
Order No. 1976

52 Weeks of Conscious Contact
Meditations for Connecting with God, Self & Others
Melody Beattie
This week-by-week guidebook will get you thinking about—and acting on—ways to bring more balance into your life. Softcover, 280 pp.
Order No. 1984

Hazelden books are available at fine bookstores everywhere. To order directly from Hazelden, call 1-800-328-9000 or visit www.hazelden.org/bookstore.